I0486745

Common Sense

for

Camera Bugs

by Richard Owen Nelson

patience may have its rewards,
but it has no guarantees

be mindful of happy accidents;
but don't brag on luck

if you pose or prep shots, admit it;
be candid if the photo is not

learn rules from others,
but don't be ruled by them

share your knowledge,
including your mistakes

keep what's worth keeping,
including <u>what not to do</u> photos

samples go farther than glances; be
generous with both

your work speaks for itself loudly;
speak softly yourself

work on improving skills and
recognizing areas for growth

don't lose too much time
trying to be someone else

courtesy and consideration
should not be ignored

don't lose your excitement
or your patience

learn rules of composition,
use them as a guide

know the rules
to know when to break them

understand what the rules provide

crop before shooting,
to increase flexibility later

there are many good books
on photography;
read or review some

learn to skim
for what you need to learn

don't get lost in the pages
and miss the lessons

use white or tan mats
for competitions

stay with simple frames

don't hide your work
with elaborate frames

don't hide your work
with colorful mats

use your own style
to present your own work
if free to do so

when entering competitions,
read and understand the rules
and determine the goals

don't imprison your photography
in a mat or frame

frames can detract from your art
while adding to cost

colored mats can detract your art
while adding to cost

the wrong color mat
can cost a sale or ribbon

the wrong color or style frame
can cost a sale or ribbon

different types of glass
can influence the impact
of your picture and presentation

learn what different tapes
do and don't do for you

consider the permanent effect
of permanent adhesive
glue / tape / mounting sheets

compare types of adhesive
removable, masking, scotch,
two-sided, adhesive,
and other tapes

Consider use of 'adhesive only'
sheets, strips, rolls, sprays

temporary adhesive
may not be what's expected

Velcro hangers can display mats
on felt type walls / panels

mat cutting is a precision work;
you need proper tools
and proper discipline

hire mat cutting and mounting
or use pre-cut mats

consider layering of mats,
and additional trim

consider what is in, out,
or to be next to your production

don't alter news photographs;
cropping is okay
some lightening is okay
some darkening is okay

don't change or spotlight the news

screens highlight with light/color
printers highlight with dark/color

media makes a difference in view

remember final destination
when doing processing

first shot after the last shot
is no shot without media

consider camera timeouts
no click is the same as no camera

flex yourself
when your equipment won't

over enable your equipment
when you're under enabled

zoom physically,
not in the camera software

fool the flash or use in daylight
to change camera's settings

get/use more resolution
for selecting subject later

use RAW when shooting
use TIFF in work flow

learn your equipment's options
and your equipment's foibles

discuss equipment with others
try loaned or rented equipment

tripods have a purpose
choose stability over pride

monopods offer stability
while keeping flexibility

'pods may hang as a pendulum,
giving balance to your camera

learn about equipment quality
research brand and outlet prices

determine acceptable delivery
of your requirements

equipment continues to improve
photos already taken do not

bags must be working gear,
not just pretty baggage

memory cards may fail;
have extras on hand;
rotate the use of supplies

learn equipment's options,
don't burden yourself with decisions

get a good rolling cutter
for smooth cuts in paper

there are many types of paper
Learn when to use what,
and for what effect

inks differ radically in life & quality

supplemental lighting
increases opportunities

flash lighting and reflectors
doesn't change what's there

trash is still trash
(which may be okay;)

don't blow your pictures out
with too much light

study the use of flash and reflectors

consider the placement of lights

shadows can enhance
as well as hide

watch for 'sprouts'
you may get a tree in an ear

props offer challenges
as well as opportunities

use props for different products
or for different projects
or to produce specific effects

straps can protect your equipment

don't let the straps
limit the equipment's use

compartmented bags
can hide as well as organize

hand grips can add to stability
yet can also detract from flexibility

filters can enhance your image
and also detract from realism
study use before experimenting

a photographer's vest is handy
don't become the focus for others

an in-camera display is nice
so is speed in getting next photo

need for speed or redisplay
changes from situation to situation

the better you know the equipment
the more you can rely on it
and the less you need to worry

refresh your equipment knowledge
gain skills on a regular interval

learn one or a few skills at a time
practice them into your memory

memorizing features won't help
if you don't recognize opportunity

keepers should have
additional backup copies

file backup on internal disk,
external disk, tape, CD's,
and memory cards are common

remote Internet backup for files
is a newer and growing option

Internet backup may have issues
such as security and timeliness;
when these are worked out,
availability will be a major asset

many sites exist for online display
not all users respect your rights

opportunities to sell your work
may be places to 'give it away'

Batteries / chargers are important
keeping a charge is ongoing task

carry extra batteries,
film, memory cards

back up your computer files;
nothing lasts forever

burnouts can't be darkened

learn to use histogram,
prevent over and under exposure

under exposure may be fixable
but it's not pleasant;
it's second best to getting it right

the better you capture the moment
the richer the rewards
without paying a price for mistakes

use macro lens for minute detail

choose lens to fit environment,
needs, and purposes

telephotos 'stack' the view,
foreground through the background

macro lens allow more detail
at the focal length of the lens

macro lens blur the rest of the view:
consider detail you want to be seen

macro lens are often built in;
macro and other lens can be added

Digital Single Lens Reflex
(DSLR) camera bodies
can have a variety of lens added;
brands differ in what fits their body

subject's motion towards the left
is considered better by many

find a market, or make one
starving is always an option

learn the ingredients
needed for archival results

criticism brings opportunities
for improvement
praise too early can bury you

friends can be enemies,
if seeking problems in work
objectivity in critiques is invaluable

get critiques independently
exhibit, compete, share

participate in learning groups

some photo printers
are more equal than others

learn the difference in printers;
ink jets, dye sublimation,
bubble jets, heat, laser,
color, black and white

consider trueness of color
and duration of print image;
consider archival needs

be careful handling prints
or stacking prints,
especially with fresh prints

with ink jet prints,
black may be slow to cure

heat and humidity affect paper,
drying time, and printer handling

one person's rules aren't 'the rule'
judges have their own bias

don't be afraid when competing
to re-enter non-winners;
they may not be losers

watch your shadow,
or see it forever

keep your back to the sun,
whenever possible

a beautiful rose is a beautiful rose;
how can *you* set it apart

what can you do
that's never been done
in the context that you are doing it

nothing new… presentation style

water drops make interesting shots

some people sprinkle flowers
to give the appearance of dew

you can 'tailor' a scene
without faking it

rivers and waterfalls
offer many aspects
of lighting, texture, shading

don't toss the silver
because it was not gold

keep the diamonds not the clay,
unless making bricks or china

reflections can
combine and separate;
try your hand at both

clouds are clouds,
unless they have
a show, a story, an effect

plan for the time of day
best for your shot

use 'sweet' time,
first / last few daylight hours

noon light can be very harsh
on your outdoor images

mid-morning and afternoon
are in the shadowlands

time can be money, or immaterial;
when is each important to you

relax on the shot at times;
let the scene capture you

junk and trash can be beautiful
market's tastes may change

value uniqueness and repetition
of shades, shapes, textures,
colors, shadows

look up and around at times,
to see the world about you

know your animal subjects:
not all geese are friendly;
squirrels are squirrelly & often nuts

know your human subjects;
be kind to those entering your view
and appearing in your viewfinder

learn about model releases
and property releases;
when needed and when not

asking for permission to an area
may gain useful tips for you,
in where and what to shoot

look for planes at airports,
boats in lakes,
trains on tracks,
but shoot such captive objects
where you see them

shoot unusual views
of ordinary items,
as well as 'common' views
on unusual items

know flowers, plants, butterflies,
bugs, trees, and their seasons

identify insects, plants, and animals
for later reference on your work;
knowing subjects give credibility

one good photo is worth
a thousand
good intentions

be a gardener in the garden:
walk, kneel, wait, and weed;
be present as an observer,
Not merely as a recorder

look up, down, and across
the rows and the scenes

don't miss what's there
just because
it's not what you set out for

the opportunities of a lifetime
are not always announced;
sometimes they have to be sought;
at times they have to be induced;
an alert eye can open the way

fog is interesting,
as much what you see
as what you don't see

find situations creating new views
or hiding old views in new images

photos in glass have many faces;
they offer the chance
to see the normal
in strange and rare places

find the best view , the best time
and the best lighting
for the result you desire…
but never ignore
what's right in front of you

a view does not 'present itself',
It is aptly discovered
by the explorer of the moment

Additional copies may be ordered
on www.Amazon.com
or www.CreateSpace.com

Search on books
by Richard Owen Nelson.

© January 12, 2008 by Richard Owen Nelson
Topeka, Kansas

www.ingramcontent.com/pod-product-compliance
Lightning Source LLC
Chambersburg PA
CBHW081246170526
45165CB00009B/3223